COULD YOU EVER SMILE WITH AXOLOTLS!?

Written by
Sandra Markle

Illustrated by
Vanessa Morales

Scholastic Inc.

For Brigid Scanlon and all the children at Parr's Ridge Elementary School in Mount Airy, Maryland.

Acknowledgments: The author would like to thank the following people for sharing their enthusiasm and expertise: Dr. Richard Griffiths, University of Kent, Canterbury, United Kingdom; Dr. Luis Zambrano, Universidad Nacional Autónoma de México, Mexico City, Mexico.

A special thank-you to Skip Jeffery for his loving support during the creative process.

Photos ©: back cover bottom left: Andrea Izzotti/Alamy Images; back cover bottom right, 1: Jane Burton/Nature Picture Library; 4: John Cancalosi/Alamy Images; 6: aureapterus/Getty Images; 8: mike lane/Getty Images; 10: Andrea Izzotti/Alamy Images; 12: Natalia Kovel/Getty Images; 14: Stephen Dalton/Avalon.red/Alamy Images; 16: Andrea Izzotti/Alamy Images; 18: mike lane/Alamy Images; 22: Andrea Izzotti/Alamy Images; 24: blickwinkel/Hartl/Alamy Images; 30 map: johnwoodcock/Getty Images; 32: Wirestock, Inc./Alamy Images. All other photos © Shutterstock.com.

Text copyright © 2026 by Sandra Markle
Illustrations copyright © 2026 by Vanessa Morales

All rights reserved. Published by Scholastic Inc., *Publishers since 1920.* SCHOLASTIC and associated logos are trademarks and/or registered trademarks of Scholastic Inc.

The publisher does not have any control over and does not assume any responsibility for author or third-party websites or their content.

No part of this publication may be reproduced, stored in a retrieval system, or transmitted in any form or by any means, electronic, mechanical, photocopying, recording, or otherwise, or used to train any artificial intelligence technologies, without written permission of the publisher. For information regarding permission, write to Scholastic Inc., Attention: Permissions Department, 557 Broadway, New York, NY 10012.

Library of Congress Cataloging-in-Publication Data available

ISBN 978-1-5461-7903-0

10 9 8 7 6 5 4 3 2 1   26 27 28 29 30

Printed in China 38
First edition, March 2026

Book design by Maria Lilja

What if one day when you woke up, you weren't quite yourself? What if your whole world had changed? What if you were in a lake living with *AXOLOTLS*!?*

*axolotls (ACK-suh-lah-tuhlz)

An axolotl is a type of salamander. Most salamanders have several stages of life: egg, larva, juvenile, and adult. But an axolotl does not have an adult stage. So, it gets bigger, older, and produces young. But it always looks and behaves like a juvenile.

An axolotl spends its whole life in water. What may look like feathery wings on its head are gills. These transfer oxygen from the water into its body. Its skin also allows it to gain more oxygen. And an axolotl has lungs. So, it sometimes gulps a little air at the surface.

An axolotl prefers to be cool. The lake in Mexico where it lives is fed by deep spring water and is rarely warmer than 68°F. During winter nights, it may drop to as low as 50°F. But it's never chilly enough to make an axolotl frown.

When you live with axolotls, playing when it's cold will never bother you.

FACT

Axolotls live in fresh water and need it to be clean.

An axolotl swims more than it walks. This motion is powered by both its strong tail and webbed feet. It's fastest when catching food or escaping enemies, such as big fish. Then it zips along at 10 miles per hour. That is faster than any champion human swimmer!

When you live with axolotls, you will race everywhere.

FACT

Axolotls have four toes on each front foot and five on each back foot, perfect for grabbing and digging.

An axolotl's body is long and skinny. Its skeleton is mostly rubbery cartilage, like human ears, and not hard bone. It can flatten its feathery gills. And its long tail is very flexible. An axolotl also has smooth skin. So, it easily bends, slips, and squeezes to get where it's going.

When you live with axolotls, you will easily take shortcuts.

FACT

Axolotls press their legs tight to their bodies when they need to be as thin as possible.

There are as many as a million axolotls in the world. But less than a thousand live in the wild. Most are cared for in aquariums. Some are studied by scientists. Many are pets. Wild axolotls are brown, gray, or green to blend into the muddy bottom and shady places of their lake home. Captive axolotls are bred to stand out. Many are white with pink gills. But the most popular axolotls also have dark speckles.

Axolotls mainly hunt at night. But keeping their eyes wide open is not a problem. Axolotls lack eyelids. That is also why they spend the daytime resting in shady places. Of course, it isn't easy to tell when an axolotl is snoozing. Or when it's awake, eyeing a possible snack.

When you live with axolotls, you might win a staring contest—if you really try.

FACT

Axolotls have poor eyesight but still smile at everything they see.

An axolotl has a keen sense of smell. Its nostrils connect to tubes containing smell sensors. But an axolotl doesn't sniff. Swimming forward pushes water through its nostrils to its smell sensors. Perfect for nighttime hunting.

When you live with axolotls, you will have fun playing Hide-and-Smell. Can you find all 5 axolotls?

FACT

Axolotls have special skin sensors that detect nearby water movements, which alert them to food or enemies.

An axolotl dines on worms, insects, and little fish. But its teeth are too tiny and dull to chomp. Instead, it opens its big mouth. Sucks food in. And swallows it whole. Its digestive system does all the work.

An axolotl usually lives alone. But when it's time to mate, a male searches until he finds a female. Then he shakes his tail and lower body in a kind of hula dance. If he wins her over, she responds by nudging him with her big snout.

When you live with axolotls, you will start a new dance craze.

FACT
Axolotls can reproduce at just 18 months old.

A female axolotl produces as many as 1,000 eggs. She sticks clusters of slime-covered eggs to plants. And she spreads out the clusters, so all her eggs are not in one place. The eggs hatch 10 to 14 days later. Then each larva must stay safe and find food on its own. It grows bigger by eating anything tiny enough to slurp up—even its brothers or sisters!

When an axolotl is injured, it heals quickly. It can even regrow a lost leg in just 40 days. The new leg starts as a bump and continues to grow until it is back to normal. Scientists are studying how axolotls do this. They suspect it is because an axolotl stays in its juvenile stage forever.

Luckily, you don't have to choose. You will always be who you are and live where people live.

WHERE DO AXOLOTLS LIVE?

In the wild, axolotls live in only one place in the whole world—Lake *Xochimilco** in Mexico. And they are in danger of disappearing there. That is because the water has become polluted, and some parts of the lake have been filled in to create small islands for farming. In those areas, there are only canals where there were once large areas of open water. The local people also introduced two kinds of fish (Asian carp and tilapia) into the lake. They were put there for people to catch, but the fish eat axolotls!

There is hope for the wild axolotl population. People have created refuges for them. They added net barriers in sections of the canals to keep out axolotl-eating fish. Also, people farming islands next to the refuges are working to keep the water pollution-free for the axolotls.

*Xochimilco (so-chee-MEEL-koh)

Lake Xochimilco, Mexico

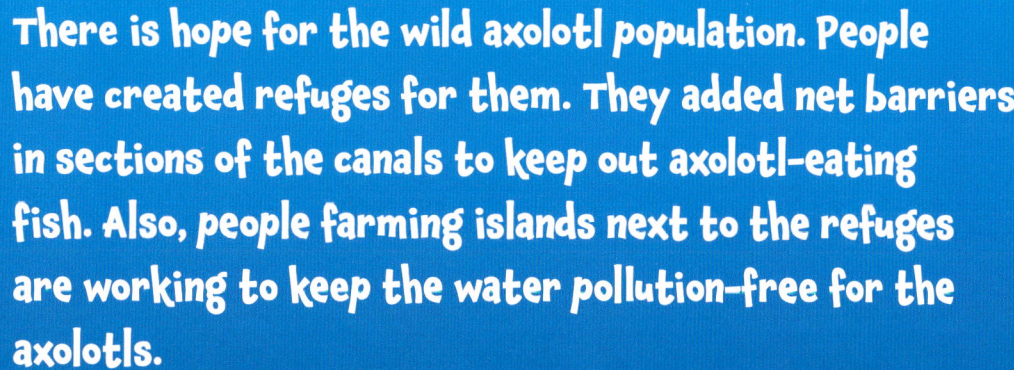

FUN FACTS!

Sometimes, an axolotl's mouth stays open for a few seconds after it swallows. That turns its usual wide grin into a smile.

The word *axolotl* comes from the ancient Aztec language Nahuatl (NAA-waa-tl) and means "water dog." They are also sometimes called Mexican walking fish. But axolotls are not fish. They are amphibians and are related to salamanders.

Axolotls can have a long lifespan, living up to 15 years in captivity. In the wild, their lives may be much shorter.

Axolotls can regrow lost body parts as often as they need to.